A Mother's Hopeless Prayer

A Mother's Hopeless Prayer

From Fear to Faith: A Newborn's Hope Against All Odds

BILLIE JO FARMER

Dirty Truth Publishing
Cleveland, Ohio
1st Edition

Published in the United States by Dirty Truth Publishing.

Library of Congress Cataloging-in-Publishing data
Names: Farmer, Billie Jo, author
Description: Cleveland: Dirty Truth Publishing (2024)
Identifiers: ISBN: (paperback) | 979-8-9898134-2-1
Subjects: Farmer, Billie Jo 1974- | Troubled Pregnancy | Infant
Medical Emergencies—United States—Biography—Women—
Cleveland

Printed in the United States of America

Cover Design: Billie Jo Farmer
Cover Photograph: Farmer family photo archives
Proofreader/Editor: Deante Young
Back Photograph: Billie Jo Farmer

First Edition, August 2024

Dedication

This book is dedicated to my beautiful grandchildren, Braylan and Harper. Nana loves you always and forever.

A special thank you to my loving partner Deante Young, who inspired me to write this book. I would have talked about it forever, but you pushed me to make it happen, so thank you.

~ *Billie Jo Farmer*

A mother's love endures through all.

~ Washington Irving ~

Contents

Prologue 9

   1. The Dream 13

   2. The Transfer 23

   3. The Pressure 33

   4. Surgery for Picc Line 43

   5. The Frightening Call 47

   6. The Next Day 49

   7. The Doctor's Visit 51

   8. The Step-Down Unit 53

   9. Going Home 57

  10. Down the Road 63

Epilogue 65

Final Thoughts:
A Plea to Expectant Mothers 69

Healing through Faith 71

More Titles 79

Prologue

A round the end of summer 1993, I started feeling nauseous and rundown. I was craving hotdogs, which I never craved before. I'm talking about hotdogs with lots of stuff on them like sauerkraut and onions, and I hated onions before that.

I took a home pregnancy test and it came back positive. I went the next day to have a blood test done, and it was negative. Next, they did a urine test, and it was positive, so I was told I was probably not far enough along for it to show in the blood test, so they sent me to a different doctor.

That doctor is the one who did the examination and said I was about eight weeks pregnant. That's when it became very serious to me. I made my first appointment within a day or two of finding out I was pregnant, and I never missed any of them.

Was I surprised? Yes and no.

Yes, because I had not missed my period. No, because of the way I had been feeling and my mom and everyone that I talked to that already had kids said, "Oh, you're probably pregnant."

Strangely enough, I continued having my period up until six months into my pregnancy.

For some women, being pregnant is a reason to celebrate. But I was just 19 years old, and I didn't know what I was gonna do. I felt joy only because any woman that gets pregnant would feel that, but at the same time, I felt a lot of sadness.

My thinking was, *how am I gonna do this? I'm not ready for kids!*

I was a very selfish person. I liked stuff for me. I wanted a lot, and it wasn't like I didn't work for things, because I did. But I always wanted everything for *me*, so how was I gonna get out of that way of thinking?

My mom was the first to know my big news, and then we called my mom's brother because my mom and I had discussed if I wasn't going to keep the baby, they would take her because they were well off financially and they loved kids.

We went back-and-forth about my uncle and aunt adopting the baby.

I only considered allowing that because I was trying to do what I thought was a good thing given my circumstances at the time. I was self-aware enough to know I didn't have a pot to piss in, no college degree and no profession other than the occasional home health care job.

Yet, there I was trying to bring a baby into the world.

I was about six or seven months along when I realized I wasn't giving my baby to my aunt and uncle. I started buying lots of baby stuff while realizing my life wasn't just about me anymore.

I followed everything the medical professionals told me to do. I didn't smoke. I didn't drink. I tried to eat everything I was told. My dedication to doing everything correctly as an expecting mother is why I never thought there would be issues with my child's health.

Doctors were more concerned that I wasn't gaining weight, than my continuing menstrual cycle. I was sick from morning to night every single day. Near the end of my second trimester, my period finally ended, and I stopped having morning sickness. I made up for lost time and began eating.

My weight went from about 145 pounds when I got pregnant, to 274 pounds at delivery.

Something was obviously wrong.

1

The Dream

I had a dream, March 16, 1994.

It was the night before I ended up in the emergency room, and it was so real. I dreamt I was sitting on the couch and heard a tapping sound on my belly. I looked down and my stomach was made of glass and a little bald-headed baby was staring up at me saying, "Mommy, please help! I'm in trouble." I woke up instantly, and my heart was racing. I went to the bathroom and splashed cold water all over my face, hoping it would take away the horrible feeling I had all over my body from the dream.

Soon after, I sat down to breakfast, and everything seemed normal, but the dream was still eating away at me. Around noon, I got into the bathtub. As I laid in the water, I noticed my belly wasn't going crazy like it usually did, which was so different. Normally, I couldn't even enjoy my bath because the baby would be jumping all over the place.

On that day, nothing.

I didn't think much of it, and I assumed the baby was sleeping. As the day went on, I felt very tired and I blamed it on being 35 weeks pregnant and huge, so of course I would be exhausted.

Then, March 17, 1994, came around. It was a new day, and I didn't have any bad dreams and even slept pretty well. I got up, did my normal routine and was back in the bathtub before I knew it. Once again, there was no movement at all from the baby, which concerned me, so I called my mom.

"I think maybe I should go to the hospital because I haven't felt any movement in the last 30 hours or so," I said to her frantically. "I'm getting scared!"

Mom said, "Okay," and we headed to the hospital.

Months before all this happened, I had found out I was pregnant at 8 weeks, and I immediately signed up for prenatal care at one of the best hospitals in Cleveland, Ohio, for babies, University Hospital. I chose them because of Rainbow Babies and Children. That facility was well known for their prenatal care, and Neonatal wing. It was also widely known because of the famous fast-food mascot, Ronald McDonald. Anytime someone went to McDonalds, they were accepting donations for the sick kids.

I wasn't impressed with that hospital's prenatal care, because I never saw the same doctor, and sometimes they would just have a nurse check me out. They forgot to do my diabetes test, and by the time they figured it all out it was too late. Of course, I was young and didn't understand the dynamics, and the

Internet was not yet a part of daily life at the time. At least, not for someone who lived paycheck to paycheck. I didn't even own a computer, so I knew nothing about any tests I was supposed to be taking at the hospital.

Mom and I arrived at the hospital, and as I walked in and told them what was going on, I was escorted to the maternity ward. A young nurse came in and checked my vitals, then told me, "Everything seems fine," and that the doctor would be in to see me.

About 20 minutes went by before the doctor showed up. In my recollection, he was a younger male doctor who pretty much did what the nurse had already done.

"I don't see any issues," he said.

He then told me to get dressed and that "a lot of first-time mothers go through emotional worries." He went on to say that I was a lot larger than most women who were 35 weeks pregnant, so my unborn child didn't have much room to move around. He also advised me to follow up with my primary OB-GYN.

I started putting my clothes back on and in walks some Asian doctor.

"Where are you going," he asked.

"The other doctor told me nothing was wrong," I said back while letting him know I was getting dressed to go home. He looked at me strangely, like I was lying.

"No. Get undressed," the Asian man said. "We are going to do an ultrasound."

I was super confused and nervous. I was like, "Okay, the other people said I was fine so it shouldn't be a big deal." He started the ultrasound and was being so quiet I felt like I needed to say something.

Breaking the uncomfortable silence, I asked, "Can you tell what the sex of the baby is?" He said absolutely nothing. Just sat with a blank stare at the screen.

Lifting myself up so I could see the screen, I asked again, "Am I allowed to know the sex of the baby?" At the same time, the doctor moved the screen away, which frightened me.

Fed up, I yelled, "What the hell is going on?"

He immediately got up and told me he would be right back. About twenty minutes later, he returned with three other people, all with a concerned look on their face. Meanwhile, I'm sick to my stomach like, *what the hell is going on*? He started the ultrasound again and they all stood there just staring at the screen with the most horrid looks on their faces. Another fifteen minutes passed, and the Asian doctor looked at me.

"Ms. Farmer, your baby is very sick and I'm not sure exactly what's wrong," he told me. "But I think maybe the baby's heart is super enlarged and we are going to send you over to a room where they can get a better look."

They wheeled me into another room which caused my mind to go crazy because I walked into that hospital, so why did I suddenly have to be wheeled over there? Anyway, I got into a room where the first things I noticed were five huge TV screens mounted to the wall. Then I saw about 10 people dressed in lab coats, all of them held clipboards and no one said anything to me.

The silence was killing me inside.

I saw a friendly face enter. "Ms. Farmer, I am the one doing this ultrasound. We moved you here so we can get a better look at what's going on," he said. "We also have all these screens, which everyone can see without piling on top of each other," he continued.

I said, "Okay."

He began the ultrasound and all I heard were whispers of concern. I kept catching glimpses of the doctors writing on their clipboards, which continued my freak out. I couldn't stand it.

Please, someone tell me what's going on, I thought to myself. That went on for almost an hour as I watched the clock slowly move. It was so quiet I could hear the tick of the clock. The guy doing the ultrasound stood up to speak.

"We are all finished Ms. Farmer. You'll be transferred to your room and the doctor will be in to see you shortly," he said. They took me back to my original room and I was like, *okay, it must have been a mistake because they are going to send me home.* Boy was I wrong.

The doctor walked in and this time, it's a woman that I didn't see any other time. She introduced herself and said:

"I have some really bad news, and I need you to please take a seat and listen because this is very important," she said.

"Ms. Farmer, your baby is very sick, and we cannot pinpoint what is really going on," she continued. "But it looks as if the baby has fluid around their heart, lungs, and stomach, which is causing it to look on the ultrasound as if the baby's heart is bigger than their chest. There's no easy way to say this, but there is no chance of survival for this baby, so we're sending you home and when you go into labor, we will deliver the baby and you will have to choose a name and then bury the baby."

The way she spoke was devastating because she offered no hope. She never said, "Hey, we can try this or that." She had zero compassion and was just as dry as a piece of burnt toast.

I cried immediately.

"Why can't you do anything? This is supposed to be the best hospital for babies. This is why I choose to get all my care here!"

The woman looked at me and said, "Calm down, you are young and healthy, you can have plenty more babies."

Can you imagine anyone telling a mother this? It was especially offensive because it came from another woman.

I flipped out with anger, knocking over the ultrasound machine and screaming at her.

"I don't want another baby! I want my baby to be fine and I'm not leaving without help." I practically begged her to take the baby out, thinking it would solve the problem. I was at my wits end and was willing to go to another hospital for a solution.

"Nobody can help you, ma'am," she said sternly. Giving you a C-section is a major surgery. Honestly, you are putting yourself at risk for a baby that isn't going to make it no matter what we do but let me talk to another doctor. I'll be right back."

My anger turned to shock in no time. I didn't know what to say or do and my mom just sat and stared at me with tears in her eyes. I asked her what she would do, and she said, "I'm sorry. I don't know, but they are the best doctors, and you should listen to whatever they say."

The doctor came back in.

"We can do a PUPS test in the morning and maybe that can tell us where the fluid is coming from," she said. "I don't want to get your hopes up because I don't see this baby having any chance of survival."

I gave her an annoyed look and said, "Okay." From that point, nothing she said was going to sit well with me because she was so insensitive and nonchalant.

I was taken to the maternity ward to get settled. A friendly young nurse walked in and said, "Ms. Farmer, I'm sorry but we have an issue. The person who does the test you need is on vacation and won't be back for two weeks, so the doctor said we are going to send you home and you can come back then."

"No! Fuck no," I yelled through a wall of tears.

"I'll just go to another hospital!"

"Give me a minute," said the friendly nurse. "Let me see what I can do."

About 30 minutes later, she returned. "I called Metro Health and they said they can do the test first thing in the morning," she said. Finally, some good news I thought, before saying, "Okay, cool! Thank you. Should I just go home and head there in the morning?"

The nurse told me to stay there and relax. "I ordered an ambulance to take you there in the morning," she added.

I was so thankful and appreciative of her. She seemed like the only one who cared. I cried all night. All I could hear was babies crying while thinking I would never hear mine cry, and that was devastating.

I was thankful they didn't put me in a room with a mother and her newborn because hearing a baby was torture enough in that situation, but seeing a mother holding her baby would have been horrible. I was in danger of never getting the chance to hold mine, hear it cry, kiss or hug my baby.

The nurse came in several times with instructions before she left. She told me the ambulance would be there between 7 a.m. and 9 a.m. and that I wasn't allowed to eat or drink anything after midnight.

I thanked her again and she left for the night.

2

The Transfer

Today is my 20th birthday, and I know it's not the best way to spend it, but I need to know what's going on with my baby. I got up to go to the restroom and when I came out, there was a breakfast tray sitting on the table. I called for the nurse, but an aide walked in.

"They told me I couldn't eat or drink anything after midnight," I said.

"Well, the nurse ordered it, so maybe there were some changes to your orders or something, the aide said.

I was like, "Okay cool," because I was hungry as hell and eight months pregnant. Plus, I hadn't eaten since the morning before.

I gobbled down what I could and drank the orange juice and chocolate milk they brought me. The ambulance drivers showed up and transferred me to Metro Health. I couldn't help but think that was the right decision because I'd never heard anything good about that hospital. Of course, Metro wasn't known for treating sick babies, and I was going stir crazy thinking about all the negatives.

When I arrived, they immediately took me to a dull, yellow-toned room that looked like it had been painted a hundred years ago. It was so ugly and spooky looking, and it had no windows and smelled musty.

None of that really mattered, though. I just wanted the doctors to figure out what was going on. A nurse walked in and hooked me up to the heartbeat monitor and was having so much trouble, she kept fumbling with it.

Great! They gave me someone who doesn't have a clue, I thought. She said, "I'll be right back." A few moments pass, and she came back with a different monitor and started fumbling again, but this time she got a faint heartbeat and suddenly, she jumped up and again told me she would be right back.

Maybe two minutes later, a different woman walked in saying she's a doctor so and so and that they needed to get me prepped for an emergency C-section. Of course, I wanted to know what was going on.

This was sudden and unexpected.

"Your baby's heartbeat is 20, and if we don't get it out ASAP, there isn't any way the baby will live," the doctor said with frightening urgency. I thought back to the UH doctor telling me this would be a major surgery and it could kill me.

All this put me in panic mode. I couldn't breathe and was freaking out like crazy, so I asked if I could go outside for a minute to clear my head. I was met with an immediate "No" because they needed to prep me as soon as possible.

A woman walked in wearing what looked like a kid's jumpsuit. She introduced herself and told me she was going to be doing the C-section, which started the tears rolling down my face.

"The other doctor said it could kill me," I said. She smiled and said, "Ms. Farmer, we do lots of C-sections every day, and I promise everything is going to be ok."

Still terrified, I asked, "What about my baby?"

"Your baby is very sick," she responded. "All I can say is we will do everything we can, but we need to get the baby out so we can work on it."

Not satisfied with her answer, I asked, "Percentage wise, what are the chances the baby will survive?" She was brutally honest when she told me the horrible estimate: "One percent."

She followed that up with something a little more reassuring: "I'm going to do everything I can to change that." As she left, the nurse looked at me and told me that doctor was the best they had. Apparently, she had been there for 40 plus hours straight and still agreed to stay.

The nurse continued, "Trust me, she is the best."

They took me to another room and had me sit on a much harder bed. The anesthesiologist said, "Okay, we are going to numb you up. I need you to bend over and grab your ankles and whatever you do, don't move." He kept sticking me in my spine and repeatedly told me he was having issues with it.

"Your spine is a little off, please hold still," he kept saying. I sat there like, *okay man. I'm huge and pregnant and I can barely grab my ankles as you requested now I gotta hold still while you're digging in my back?* I tell myself to stop that way of thinking and *get yourself together and let them tend to your baby as fast as they can.*

Once he finally finished, they placed me on another bed and walked me down the hallway. A nurse approached us asking if they should resuscitate if my baby is born not breathing. My first instinct was, No! I don't want my baby to suffer, so I signed the "Do Not Resuscitate" form and as soon as they moved me onto the final bed where I was going to have the C-section, I asked, "Can I change my mind?"

The doctor looked at me confused and says, "About what?"

"I want them to do everything they can to save my baby," I said.

"Normally (you can't change your mind), but let me get another paper," the doctor said as she sent the nurse out. When she ran back in, I signed the paper and finalized it: "do everything you can to save my baby."

The C-section began and I was still having horrible anxiety. I couldn't even feel myself breathing. I asked them if they were sure I was breathing and after about ten times asking, one of the doctors said, "Yes, or you wouldn't be talking so much."

"You're not supposed to feel anything," the doctor said. "Trust me, you don't want to feel it."

I felt a bunch of tugging and pulling, and I heard the doctor say, "This baby is so stubborn, we need to cut again!" She looked over the sheet and said, "We need to cut another spot. The baby is holding their foot like they don't want to come out."

A few minutes pass, and I hear the baby is out and I see people running all over the place.

I don't hear anything else, so I repeatedly ask, "Is my baby okay?"

Finally, the doctor looked in my direction and told me they were working on her, and it hit me that she said "her" this time. She said, "I'm closing you up Ms. Farmer; did you have a named picked out for your daughter?"

I said, "Yes. Bethany Renee," and my aunt, who was standing behind me said, "How about Bethany Faith, since she needs all the faith she can get?" I said, "Okay, fine. I just want to see my baby."

The doctor said, "Honey, she has been rushed to the neonatal unit and they are working on her." I asked if she was alive and she told me they were able to resuscitate her, but "she is very sick."

They promised to keep me updated.

I felt kind of relieved but scared at the same time. It was weird because it felt as if she might be ok. The next thing I remember is them wheeling me out of the operating room and into a nicer room and I must have fallen asleep. It was late when I opened my eyes, and I immediately rang the bell for the nurse.

The nurse came in. "I want to see my baby," I said.

"Well first, we need to get you up to urinate and make sure you are okay," she said. So, I started to sit up, and she said, "No! Slowly."

Me being hardheaded, I jumped up and boy, was that the wrong thing to do. I instantly fell back onto the bed in excruciating pain.

"I told you slowly," she said.

I went to the bathroom to urinate and got instantly freaked out again.

I'm bleeding down there, so I screamed and rang the bell for the nurse, and she ran into the room. I told her I was hemorrhaging, and she said, "Honey that's not a lot of blood." I said, "You don't understand. I had a C-section and I'm not supposed to bleed from there!"

I never seen someone laugh so hard. She said, "Girl, yes you are. When you have a baby, no matter where you have it from, you bleed."

I was too much in a rush to even be embarrassed. I said, "Whatever! Can I go see my daughter?" She says, "Well, we are short staffed, so it's going to be a little bit."

Now I'm pissed.

I'm like, What the hell? My baby is sick! I just want to see her. One would think that you would want the mom right by her baby's side especially at a time like this.

An hour passes, and in walks a preacher. "Ms. Farmer, I just left from seeing your daughter, and I came up to ask if you would like me to baptize her?" he asked. I said, "Yes of course! But I want to be there." He told me there wasn't much time. The nurse said it may be hours before they can get someone to take me down and they weren't sure if my daughter would survive that long.

How dumb does that sound to you? I couldn't go see my dying daughter because they were short staffed.

I instantly rang the bell for the nurse. I looked at the preacher and said, "Yes. Please go ahead and I'll be down shortly." The nurse came in and asked with an attitude, "Yes Ms. Farmer?" I know she was listening to what I said to the preacher.

"I want to go see my daughter now," I said firmly. She tried to throw me the same BS, so I asked for a wheelchair. I decided I was going right then and there.

She huffed and puffed out the room in a fit. Within moments, she returned and told me she would have one of the aides take me down, which happened right away. They had me check in at the front desk in the NICU and sent me immediately to the wash table to scrub my hands.

My thoughts: *Screw all this, I just want to get to my baby.* The aide turned the wheelchair around and pushed me to a small bed that looked different than the others.

This wasn't an incubator. This was like a small open baby bed, but it was up so high, I couldn't even see what, if anything, was in it. I stood up and the shock to my eyes was my baby lying flat on her back, legs sprawled out but sideways almost. Her arms were strapped down with all these tubes in them and one down her throat. I almost passed out because I couldn't believe what I was seeing.

I looked to the side and asked the woman who took me down, "Are you sure this is my baby?" and she said, "Yes, I'm so sorry."

A nurse walked over and said, "Hi Ms. Farmer, I am your daughter's nurse." I said, "Hi, can you please let me hold her?"

She said, "No, I'm sorry. Your daughter is very sick, and nobody can pick her up. She has a lot of tubes in her."

I'm crying so hard I could barely see. I asked, "Is she going to make it?"

The nurse said, "I can't answer that. All I can say is we will do everything we can to help her."

Unwilling to accept her words, I said, "I can stay here with her."

The aide answered, "No. I have to take you back up in a few minutes." I was so angry that I just wanted to scream.

Why couldn't I stay with my baby? That's what I wanted to scream to them, but I went along with their suggestion. "Please go get some rest, and if anything happens, I will personally come get you," the nurse said, trying to put me at ease.

The aide took me back up and the preacher was there waiting. He was holding a little card with a seashell in it with my daughter's name and birthdate. It also indicated she had been baptized. He told me that my mother was there when he did it. "I didn't see her when I went down," I said.

He told me she went to the cafeteria to get something to eat and wanted me to have time alone with Bethany.

For the rest of the night, I rang the nurse about every 30 minutes asking to be taken back down to see my baby. I kept being told they were short staffed, except for the one time I was told, "You were lucky to have gone earlier."

Of course, I told her what I thought of her nasty attitude. I think that was the longest night of my life, even more than the night before, because I at least had my baby next to me in my stomach.

3

The Pressure

I woke up after a few hours of sleep and I instantly rang for the nurse. She walked in and I was happy to see it was a different nurse.

Thank God!

That thankfulness lasted a whole ten seconds. I said, "Hi, can I please go see my baby?" The new nurse hit me with a, "No. We are short staffed…" I instantly cut her off and said, "I don't want to hear that bullshit today! I can take myself, please just get me a wheelchair."

She told me I couldn't.

I demanded she get me the papers I needed to sign myself out.

She turned and walked out without a word said.

I sat there thinking she was coming back with the papers to let me sign myself out and an hour passes and nothing, so I rang the bell again and she came over the speaker and said the doctor was on the floor and will be in soon.

About 20 minutes pass, and in comes a doctor full of energy and smiles. I'm thinking, *okay, this doctor is cool and is going to let me go.*

Nope. He says, "Ms. Farmer, you just had a major surgery. I cannot let you leave." I explained what was going on and how they wouldn't let me go see my baby. He smiles and says, "Ok, here's the deal: if you can get up and walk around the tower four times without stopping, I'll let you sign an AMA and you can leave."

I instantly say, "Okay, let's go!"

Keep in mind, this hospital has two towers, and each one is for different types of floors. Mine of course, is the maternity ward. It has about 25 rooms in a circle to make a complete pass, that's just a guess, but whatever. I'm about to show him I can do it so I can leave and go downstairs to be with my baby girl.

I had been here one whole day which includes the C-section and overnight stay. This is around noon the next day and not one family member or friend has come to my room so I'm a wreck.

I'm like, *what is going on?* I was butt hurt because I was all alone.

The doctor walked out, and I heard the nurse ask him, "Why did you tell her that?" He said, "Because she will never be able to do it and it will shut her up." My evil laugh came out and I whispered to myself, "Okay smart ass, watch me." The nurse came in and disconnected the IV.

"Let's see if you can do this," she said. "I'm going to give you a wheelchair to brace yourself on."

I'm so furious and eager to prove a point, I said, "Don't bother. I got this."

I started walking and passed about three rooms.

The pain was ungodly.

I'm wanting to sit to make the pain go away.

For the record, they never offered me anything for pain at this point, but I was determined. *This is a one-shot deal; don't blow it,* I say to myself. As I strode painfully around the floor, I focused on every room I walked past and not the pain I was feeling.

I looked at pictures.

I looked at people.

I heard a scattered assortment of sounds around me all while saying to myself, *keep going. You've got this.*

I made it three times around and as I passed my nurse, she said with a giggle, "Oh, I see you got a high pain threshold." I ignored her and kept going. As my final lap ended, I saw her sitting at the desk across from my room.

I smirked and said, "Please get the doctor. I'm ready to go now."

I walked back into my room and sat on the bed wanting to cry from all the pain, but I'm like *don't do it. Never let them see you cry in pain, or he will go back on the deal.*

About 20 minutes passed and in comes the doctor with the AMA paper to sign. He says, "You do know if anything including death happens to you after this, it's your own fault, correct?" I told him I had no problem with that.

The nurse came in with a wheelchair and asked if she could wheel me down.

"Don't bother," I snapped. "If you are short staffed, I wouldn't want to inconvenience anyone."

I walked right past her and got on the elevator headed down to the NICU. This was the longest walk I had ever taken. Not really, but it sure felt like it.

I walked up to the NICU receptionist and told her my name. She handed me a pass to get in, and I walked over to scrub in, and I saw my mother and my daughter's father's mother standing by my baby. Both women looked at me like, "What the hell are you doing?"

I said, "I'm fine. Thanks for asking." I was a little butt hurt that none of them even bothered to call up and ask if I was okay or if they could come up and bring me down to see my daughter. But I was thankful as well because they were there with my baby when I couldn't be. My mother later explained that she was scared to talk to me because she didn't want to hear me crying.

It would've broken her heart and she did call the nurse multiple times and they said I was sleeping, which I doubt they were telling her the truth because I barely slept. "It's okay," I said.

"I'm just glad you were able to be there for Bethany."

They both said they would step out and let me spend some alone time with her. The same nurse from the day before walked toward us, greeted me, then instantly started telling me how they didn't think my baby would make it through the night. She also told me I had "a little fighter" on my hands and that her "heart breaks" for me because she couldn't imagine the pain I was feeling.

A few minutes went by, and a doctor walked over. She greeted me and said, "Ms. Farmer, I would like you to come into the conference room and sit down with me so we can chat."

This didn't sound good at all.

We walked in and I sat down.

"You do realize your daughter is very sick and we do not expect her to make it," she said. I said, "Yes. I've been told this several times, but she is here so what can you do to help her?"

"We are doing everything in our power," the doctor claimed. "The problem is we don't know why this happened. Bethany weighed 7 pounds, 4 ½ oz, but we think at least one pound of that was fluid because she was five weeks early.

Then, the questions start.

"Did you drink alcohol while pregnant?"

"Did you use drugs while pregnant?"

"Did you smoke cigarettes while you were pregnant?"

All my answers were a flat "No."

She continued.

"What were the results of your HIV test?"

I said, "Negative!"

She said, "OK. We are going to run another one on you and your daughter."

"Whatever you need, I'm all for it," I said.

She continued, "We are having consults with doctors from Duke University about a baby they had born with similar issues, and they will possibly fly in to help the team out." She went on to tell me that in all her years being a doctor, she never saw a baby so sick and remain alive.

"We will have to insert a PICC line because your daughter's veins keep collapsing and she needs an open line for treatment," the doctor said.

Feeling scared, but knowing it was necessary, all I could say was, "Okay, fine. Do whatever you have to, because I don't know what a PICC line is, but you're the doctor."

"Bethany currently has three chest tubes, two on one side and one on the other and we change them every eight hours," the doctor said. "Right now, the fluid is coming out so fast that it's full every time they change them. She also has a tube in her throat to breathe for her because currently, she is not breathing at all on her own."

This was overwhelming. I knew I wasn't going to remember all those important details.

"I'm sorry, but I'm so confused and just completely thrown away with all this," I said to the doctor. "It's a lot."

She told me she understood.

"Please, whatever you need for me to do just say it and it will be done," I said to her. "Does she need blood? An organ? What?"

The doctor said, "Unfortunately, you cannot give her anything because she doesn't have your blood type." She told me she spoke to Bethany's dad's mother, and she informed her that her son wouldn't be a good fit and she would leave it at that.

With a very concerned look on her face, the doctor asked, "Do you know what she meant by that? Is he the father?"

I knew I had to clarify things. "He is 100 percent the father and she meant that because he's an addict."

"Oh, I see," said the doctor. "Well, we can get everything she needs like blood and platelets from the Red Cross. It's not a problem." I needed the doctor to be honest with me, so I had to ask a difficult question.

"Yesterday, the other doctor said Bethany's chances of survival was maybe one percent," I said nervously. "Is that a true guess?"

"I wouldn't even give it that, Ms. Farmer," she said. "I am completely surprised she was even able to be resuscitated, but she was and all we can do is hope for the best but expect the worst."

I had to ask.

"If she does make it, is she going to be sick all the time like this?"

The doctor said, "We would never know that ahead of time, but I can tell you there were seven other babies born before her with this medical issue, and only one other baby survived…"

That felt hopeful, until she finished her thought. "He is blind and deaf, and he cannot walk or talk and has many other issues." That was the moment I started doubting myself. I couldn't help the thoughts running through my mind:

You made a mistake. You should've never asked to change the "Do Not Resuscitate" papers.

She is going to suffer her entire life, why would you do that?

She doesn't deserve to go through this pain...

I felt like I was being selfish and just wanted her here because that's what I wanted, not thinking of the pain she would have to endure the rest of her life.

"Do you know how long she will have to stay in here if she does pull through," I asked the doctor. I'm not sure I liked her brutal honesty when she said, "If she pulls through, she will have to stay at least six months, but please do not get your hopes up."

Moments later, I walked back out to my baby. That's when the true praying started. I prayed the day before, but there I was begging God, "If she's going to suffer, please just take her now. I don't want her feeling any more pain at all."

As I stood over her with tears pouring, thinking I made a huge mistake I couldn't fix, I stared at her. My baby was beautiful to me, but the truth was painful. She looked so deformed — not even human. She practically looked make believe, swollen from fluid and her ears stuck way out from her head, which was abnormally shaped, almost like an alien.

Her legs wouldn't close. Her belly was huge with fluid and so many tubes were coming from everywhere.

But she was fighting, and I had to pray she wasn't suffering.

4

Surgery for Picc line

ast night was rough. I got to see for the first-time doctors changing my baby's chest tubes. My God, that was the worst thing. She trembled and shook; the nurse said it was very painful because they had to break her ribs to get through. I can't really remember, but I think it was because she was a baby and not as much room for placement. I just sat and thought, *how in the world does this little baby take that much pain, and live?*

The time had come. I was told I could walk down with my baby, but I couldn't go into the operating room. I didn't like that because I didn't want to leave her side at all. As we walked down, they were using an AMBU bag to keep her breathing until they got to the operating area.

Once we made it, they didn't have a room ready, so they moved her and us to a waiting area and said it might be a 10-minute wait. They hooked her up to a portable machine to get her back on the ventilator, and the plug didn't work. They pushed people in beds out of the way, scrambling to find another outlet and everyone was frantic because the nurse with the AMBU bag left with it.

People were screaming for other nurses to help. I was freaking out because I didn't truly understand what was going on, but I saw their fear, which transferred to me.

After about two or three minutes (which seemed like 20), they found a plug and got her hooked up. Is this a sign that she shouldn't have this surgery done, I wondered. I decided to just keep praying. The O.R. nurse came out to say, "Ok, we are ready for her." I cried as they wheeled her back, not knowing if she would even survive surgery.

She was still so very sick.

An hour or so passed, and the medical staff came to tell me the surgery went well, the PICC line was in, and my daughter was in recovery. I was asked to give them a few minutes before being taken back to see her. After a half hour wait, I went up to the lady at the desk.

The look on her face terrified me.

"I'm sorry, but your daughter is back in the NICU," she said.

I'm like, "What the hell? They said they would come get me!" She shrugged her shoulders and directed me to the NICU.

As I headed back there, I couldn't help but wonder if something bad happened and they forgot to tell me what was going on. When I arrived in the NICU, I immediately saw my baby. The nurse walked over and said she came through it fine. Everything was working properly, and it was a success.

As the night went on, it seemed as if the fluid was starting to disappear, and she was filling out more. Her ears didn't seem to stick out as much and she would move a little when she heard loud beeping.

"Is that normal," I asked the nurse. She said it was a good sign because it meant my baby was responding to sounds. Before, she had no response at all after the surgery and they were a little concerned.

I could tell that nurse truly cared for my daughter. She was so attentive and the look in her eyes when she was taking care of her just looked so caring. Her name was Kim. I'm so frustrated I can't remember her last name, but we are talking 30 years ago.

As the days went on, Bethany had her ups and downs, but she held her own. I was eventually allowed to hold her for the first time at three weeks old, an eternity for a mother. I clearly remember the first bath I gave her because I was so nervous! She still had all these tubes in her and I was scared I was going to hurt her.

Nurse Kim was by my side saying encouraging words, but she had bathed her before.

I was going home every night by then, because my baby was doing much better. They kept telling me to go because I never let my own body heal and I always looked pale. They told me Bethany had a long road to recovery and that she would be there at least six months.

Every day, they advised me to rest while I could.

5

The Frightening Call

"Get up here now," my mom screamed to me.

Bethany was about 4 ½ weeks old, and I had been at the hospital most of the day and went home to shower. As soon as I got out and heard my mother's blood curdling scream, I ran upstairs to where she was.

Bethany's nurse was on the phone.

"We need you to come as fast as you can," she said urgently. "We don't know what's going on, but the fluid has just stopped coming out and we're doing X-rays to see where it was going."

I slammed the phone down. Metro was about 25 minutes from where I lived, but I made it there in about ten. I broke every law imaginable and didn't care how fast I was going.

I was going to get there quickly.

When I rushed into the NICU, the nurse came up and said Bethany was doing okay, but they couldn't figure out why the fluid just stopped. They were scared it was going somewhere else, but all the tests showed it just stopped.

That was good news to me, so why was she so excited in a bad way?

The nurse explained they were not sure if one of the chest tubes clogged up, so they changed every one of them and did the X-rays and found nothing. A CT scan showed nothing, so they were in disbelief that the fluid that poured out every day all day had stopped.

The doctor told us he didn't know what was going on.

We had to keep repeating the test and watch my baby very closely through the night. Of course, I wasn't going home, so I pulled up a chair and held her hand all night, and it was a long one. I sat in a chair with my arm holding her little hand and a couple of times, she squeezed my finger.

It was the best feeling ever. She had her ups and downs, but she pulled through.

6

The Next Day

The fluid still hadn't returned, but the doctors seemed to have calmed their worry down. I sat there most of the day and Bethany was doing well. She was moving around a lot and didn't seem to be stressed, so I told the nurse that I was going home to shower, and I would be back in a couple hours.

I took that long walk back to the parking garage and got into my car and was rushing to get home and shower, so I could get back there as quickly as possible. I walked in the house, and I heard my mom yelling from upstairs that the hospital called.

I ran back to the car and my heart was pounding out of my chest. I was speeding and crying, because I just needed to get back.

I must describe the trip because it's not just a hop and a skip.

It's at least a 25-minute ride even while speeding with no traffic. I also had to park in the parking garage which meant get a ticket and find a space, then I had to walk across the overpass, which was maybe 1200-1500 feet across.

I had to walk almost to the back of the hospital and take the elevator, which wasn't moving as fast as I wanted. I was going stir crazy wondering what in the hell happened so fast.

Once in the NICU, I went over to Bethany's bed, and she was fine.

One thing stood out: She didn't have the tube down her throat anymore, which made me wonder what happened. The nurse walked up and said Bethany decided to pull the tube out that was helping her breathe, I'm thinking, *okay why didn't you put it back in?*

I didn't realize it could damage her vocal cords.

Placing it in and doing it a second time was riskier, so they wanted to monitor her for a while to see if she could breathe in a regular incubator that pushed out less oxygen.

I said, "Okay," but the nurse told me I could request for it to be put back in. I said, "No. If they want to try this, let's do it." Who wants to risk damaging their kid's vocal cords?

I sat there the rest of the night and Bethany was breathing fine on her own. The next day, the doctor came to see me.

7

The Doctor's Visit

The doctor pulled me into the conference room.

This is never good.

She said, "Ms. Farmer, you have a very strong daughter. She managed to pull the tube completely out and hold it in her hand like she wanted to hand it to us! I've only seen one other baby do that, and he was nowhere near as sick as Bethany, so I don't know where she got the strength, but she did it."

The doctor continued: "While I have you in here, the results came back from you and Bethany's HIV test."

I'm like, *oh my God, I had forgotten about that.*

They never said anything, so I assumed it was okay. "They were both negative," she said. "We also checked your blood for drugs and diseases, and we found nothing." At that point, Bethany's illness was *Hydrops Fetalis* (non-immune), but we still had no idea why this happened.

It may always be a mystery.

I asked, "What's that?" She said, "It's a very serious condition that almost always leads to death, and it's a buildup of fluid around the heart, lungs, and under the skin."

She went on to say that its causes are viral infections, heart disease, and chromosomal abnormalities. Hematological causes and autoimmune causes, but we couldn't find any of those wrong, so we just didn't know.

"Is she going to be okay," I asked.

She said, "We don't know. She will probably be blind, deaf, or never walk or talk. We won't know until later. We also don't know if the fluid will ever start again or not, it's pretty much a wait and see." She went on to say that if Bethany made it to 18 years old, she should be okay and that the risks decrease with every year she lives.

As a mother, those chances seemed devastating, but I had to remember that she made it through surgery and managed to pull the breathing tube out and she was still here. Whatever we had to deal with, we could do it.

Bethany continued to improve and was moving around more and more each day. She struggled to eat because she went so long with a tube feeding her, she had lost the sensation to suck.

8

The Step-Down Unit

Bethany was transferred to the step-down unit at five weeks, and she continued to improve more and more each day. She had a very hard time with the speech therapy to teach her to suck the nipple as most babies can do right from birth.

The therapist said that it was normal for babies as sick as she was to struggle. I don't think I left at all from the step-down unit room because I felt like I would get home and be called right back, so obviously she didn't want me to leave.

My mom brought me clothes, and I washed up in the bathroom. On the third day being in the step-down unit, the nurse walked in.

"I'm washing up," I said.

She said, "Why?"

"Because I'm dirty," I responded.

She told me they had showers for parents, which would have been nice to know weeks earlier. On Day 4, they decided to take the PICC line out.

The nurse said, "You mean the CVC line?" I had no clue what these things were called. I just went by what they told me downstairs.

They took out the CVC line, and a piece of tubing broke off Bethany's neck. I saw the whole imprint of the small piece of tube, but it looked huge because she was small.

Great. Another issue.

They brought the doctor up. "It will be okay. She will keep an eye on it, but it should be fine."

I was looking at a tube like, *no it's not fine,* and he says, "We can take her in for surgery and remove it, but she may be back on the ventilator…"

I interrupted and asked, "What else can you do?"

He said, "Well, we can leave it for now and let her heal. If it's bothering her or it starts growing scar tissue when she gets older, we can remove it then."

Okay whatever. I'm pissed, but what other option did I have but surgery, which would risk her getting the ventilator back?

Days five and six, Bethany seemed to be doing so much better. She was taking and eating a full bottle without issues so the doctor came in and said, "Okay, tomorrow, Bethany can go home."

I was super pumped because I was told that would take at least six months if she even survived.

9

Going Home

My mom brought over the beautiful outfit Bethany's aunt Lorie got her for Easter, but of course, she couldn't wear it at the time.

I decided it would be her going home outfit.

The dress was cute with pastel-colored ruffles on it. I got her all dressed up, looking so beautiful and I was excited to finally go home and be a mom. As we were leaving, many doctors and nurses came to say goodbye.

Of course, the best nurse was Kim.

She stood right by my daughter's side and became super emotional anytime something happened to her. Bethany's main doctor came up to me and said she never believed in miracles until she met Bethany.

"That baby went from me not expecting her to live for an hour, let alone be going home at 6 weeks," she said. The doctor also told me she wouldn't ever forget her and to "please make sure" I bring her by for them to see her on occasion.

Our discharge papers indicated we had to take Bethany to the eye doctor that day. That threw me for a loop.

I just wanted to take my baby home, but whatever.

It was right across the street in their doctor office building. We walked there and checked in to the eye clinic and I was told to have a seat. It was still early, around 1 p.m., but it wasn't until about 3 p.m. when they called us back.

As we headed back, I wasn't thinking anything other than it's just an appointment.

We walked into the tiny office and the doctor said, "Oh hi. So, this is the little miracle baby I've heard so much about!" He asked if I knew why they scheduled that appointment.

"No. I just found out as we were leaving," I said.

"I assumed it was a normal visit."

The doctor explained that he had seen Bethany a couple weeks prior, and her eyes were in bad shape then.

I was so caught off guard. I blurted, "Oh no! Nobody told me this."

The doctor told me he was sorry no one told me, but he wanted to see how she was doing being off the ventilator. He explained that babies on ventilators, especially at 100% for long periods of time, usually go blind or have serious issues from it.

He placed what looked like paper clips on Bethany's eyes. Immediately, the reflexes of my six-week-old baby caused her to almost whip the doctor. He called in a nurse, and I had to help hold her down so they could get them on her.

It was heartbreaking to see her like that, but I knew it had to be done.

He finished and said, "Well, no improvement at all. I will need to see Bethany once a week so we can keep checking to see if there is any progress, but she may never be able to see."

I was emotionally exhausted and numb.

That super-happy day turned devastating. I went back to second guessing myself after I felt so relieved, *I don't want my baby to be blind, God please help her!* Then, I wiped my tears and told myself to be thankful.

I needed to be thankful God had gotten her that far, and she was such a fighter, that she would pull through that too. We headed home, and on the way, I kept praying, "Please God, let her be okay."

I was happy to take her home, but I became super nervous. What if she stops breathing? What if I fall asleep and wake up and she has passed away? There were so many racing thoughts that I was sure any mother would've had in that situation.

When we finally got home, the phone didn't stop ringing. The visiting nurse wanted to stop by, and I'm like, "Seriously today?"

She said, "Well, yes. Your staples were supposed to be out last week, and I need to check on the baby and her living conditions…"

"Ok, whatever. Come on," I said.

When she came by and asked if she could take care of me first, I stared at her.

"I already removed my staples," I told her.

She yelled, "What?"

"Look, they were snagging on my pants and ripping, and I didn't have time to go to the doctor or wait for you, so I grabbed a pair of pliers and took them out."

"Oh my God! I never heard of anybody doing something that dumb," she said.

"Let me see the incision marks. I bet they are infected."

She slowly pulled the front of my pants down and told me she was "quite impressed." She told me they weren't infected and seemed to have already healed.

I had more important things on my mind.

"Okay, now let's talk about Bethany," I said.

"When did you stop the drugs," she responded.

I said, "Excuse me?"

"Isn't that why Bethany was born five weeks early," she boldly asked.

"Um, no. She was sick, and I don't appreciate you assuming that bullshit," I shot back.

She tried apologizing once she read the baby's chart, but I told her to get out. I planned to have other nurses come to replace her. She handed me a paper with several dates on it. "Well, at least let me give you this," she said. "I made all of Bethany's appointments for the next two weeks for you."

I looked at the paper and OMG! She had appointments every day but Saturday and Sunday, Lord help me. Bethany had to be seen in the eye clinic, the regular pediatrician, nutrition, speech therapy, the special needs clinic and of course, they were not all on the same day. In fact, they were one a day.

Okay, maybe we should have just stayed in the hospital.

Over the next few weeks, my mother and I took her to the appointments, and if they began at 8:30 am, we didn't leave until 5 pm when they were locking the doors. I never saw so much overbooking in my life, but we got through it. Bethany had appointments like that every week for probably six weeks, then they slowed down.

Except for the eye doctor.

Bethany's eyes were improving each time we went, but she was still legally blind in one eye. The doctor began seeing her sometimes twice a week, and she had the highest doses of morphine they could give a baby because of the chest tube changings.

When she came home, if it wasn't completely silent in the house, she would scream and shake horribly. I'm not going to lie, that was rough, and it stayed that way for probably six months or more.

If the phone rang, she screamed. If I sneezed, she screamed. Nobody could watch TV, turn on the microwave, or anything.

10

Down the Road

After about eight months, she was getting better and better, even though she was still a little off on her development. The doctor seemed to think she would catch up. Her eyes improved around maybe a year old, and she only needed to see the eye doctor once a year.

At her second-year eye appointment, the doctor said she had almost perfect vision and he didn't see any reason to come back, unless she was having issues. He told us he had never seen a baby's eyes reverse themselves without surgery when they were that bad.

A few months later, Bethany had an appointment with her pediatrician, and I asked her why the tube from the CVC line that was left in her, seemed to be growing. The pediatrician looked and said, "Well, there is scar tissue growing around it, but it could be something more, so we need to get her into surgery and get that taken out as soon as possible.

About a week later, she had surgery to remove the tube.

The surgery was a success, according to the doctor, but he became concerned when it appeared to be more than scar tissue. It was sent off to be tested and we were told we would know something in about two weeks.

Please Lord, this baby can't take anymore, I was saying to myself.

The test results came back in a week, and it was finally great news. There was only scar tissue in the tube, nothing else. But by the time Bethany was 3 years old, she started running into things and saying her eyes hurt so I scheduled a doctor's appointment.

I wasn't too concerned because she was a kid and sometimes things like that happen. At the appointment, one of her eyes was getting bad again so she had to wear a patch over the other eye.

We were trying to find out if the bad eye would strengthen, which was horrible and uncomfortable. Imagine trying to get a 3-year-old to keep wearing an irritating patch.

Two weeks later, her glasses came in and I was told to let her pick the frames because she would more than likely wear them if she liked them. It turns out she did wear them more than I think she would've had I picked them out, but it was still a struggle to get her to wear them consistently.

At her appointment the following year, her eyes once again reversed themselves and she was back to almost perfect vision.

Epilogue

O ver the years, Bethany was super healthy, vibrant, and so full of energy. It was such a joy to see that baby go from a less than one percent chance of making it, to being healthy with no issues whatsoever. I had to send praise to God because I never got on my knees and prayed so hard for anything ever in my life, and it just had to be a miracle from God.

Bethany is 30 years old as of 2024 and she is the mother of two beautiful children, Braylan, and Harper, and they are my pride and joy. When she got pregnant with Braylan, of course I was beyond scared that this might happen to him, and I'm sure she was too, but the doctors assured us that it probably wouldn't.

She had a few issues during the delivery that ended in a C-section, but no major complications.

We were so grateful.

Her delivery with Harper was a planned C-section, and it went smoothly without complications.

So this baby, born March 18, 1994, with a maybe one percent chance of living, is now a mostly healthy 30-year-old with two children of her own. She does have a disease called IIH

(Idiopathic Intracranial Hypertension), and her doctors say it has nothing to do with the issues at birth.

I'm sure she will have her struggles with this illness over the years, but it will never amount to the pain she had to endure as a newborn. I can say that not only have I met the strongest person in the world, but I gave birth to her.

The purpose of me writing this book is to leave my daughter and grandchildren a recollection of the details from someone who was there daily. I think it's important for her children to know how their mom fought to be here and how the power of prayer and a set of wonderful doctors and nurses helped her to give birth to them.

I also wanted to write this book for all mothers who have or will receive news their baby is sick or has a medical issue. You must pray like never before, and never take the word of one doctor who says your baby isn't worth it.

Fight for your children and don't give up.

Don't be afraid to speak up, even if you're cussin' like a sailor.

A child has no one to speak for them but their parents.

I often cry when I think back to that time. What if I had walked out the door of University Hospital and went home, instead of standing my ground?

What would have happened?

Would Bethany have survived?

Would I have survived?

I can assure you Bethany wouldn't have survived, and I probably wouldn't have either.

One of the doctors at Metro said the fluid on Bethany's head would have crushed her skull and thrown me into shock and possibly killed me as well if I had a vaginal delivery.

I see so many mothers online saying they are pregnant, and their doctor says there's "no hope." I even saw one who said her doctor suggested aborting.

Please read my story and keep the faith. I'm not saying that to get anyone's hopes up, thinking that "oh her baby survived, so will mine." Unfortunately, that won't always be the case, but keep in mind your baby deserves a fighting chance and the only person who can fight for them is you.

A mother will always get that gut feeling: a mother's intuition. Go with that and never let anyone tell you differently.

I want to give special thanks to the wonderful doctors and nurses at Metro Health Medical Center and especially the ones in the NICU. I'm sorry I don't remember all their names, but I can say they were truly the best and God put me in the right place and my daughter in the right hands.

Final Thoughts

A Plea to Expectant Mothers

O ver the years, I've done a lot of second-guessing about the decisions I made in the hospital choice I made and not questioning things doctors and nurses neglected to do. Never seeing the same doctor and everyone seeming clueless was an unacceptable mess.

My first incident was the ultrasound at four months, which in 1994 was given once unless they found something wrong. I showed up with my bladder full as instructed, but due to an emergency, I was left sitting for almost two hours. I approached the receptionist and asked how much longer it would be because I felt like my bladder was going to explode.

She instructed me to go to the bathroom and let a little pee out and they would be with me shortly. I went to the bathroom, but as I'm sure anyone who has held their pee for two hours can understand, not just a little bit comes out.

A lot does.

I drank more water, but the tech called my name shortly after. I explained what happened and she said, "It should be okay." She started the ultrasound and kept saying it was very hard to see but didn't see anything abnormal.

It was there I should have demanded another ultrasound, but I trusted they did things in my best interest, so I accepted that.

The second incident was at about the fifth month when one of the doctors asked me if they had given me the RhoGAM shot at my first appointment.

Confused, I said, "I have no clue what that is, but I never got a shot anytime here."

The last one occurred at my final appointment, about a week before Bethany was born. A doctor asked me if I had taken the glucose test because she couldn't find the results, which confused once again.

I still had no clue what that was she told me it didn't matter because by then, it was too late to take it. "You would have remembered it because you have to drink some nasty liquid," she said.

My advice to pregnant women: make sure you read up on everything, especially tests that need to be performed. Don't be afraid to repeatedly ask questions about what needs to be done or why it hasn't been done. Never assume everything was done that needed to be.

Summary Report

Baby's Name: Bethany Faith Murray
Baby's Unit #: 1005613
Mother's Name: Billie Farmer, 812 E. 156th Street- up, Cleveland, Oh 44110
Mother's Unit #: 389810
Phone #: (216) 851-6509
Admitting Attending: Robin Benis, M.D.
Discharge Attending: Robin Benis, M.D.

Admission Information:

Birth History: 20 year old G2, P1, AB1 mother. Prenatal ultrasound-diagnosed with polyhydraminos, hydrops, bilateral pleural effusion. Delivered by c-section. Required CPR in delivery room. Had bilateral thoracentesis-improved-transferred to NICU.

Maternal Blood type: A positive   *Infant Blood type*: O negative

Admitting Diagnoses: 1) Hydrops Fetalis (non-immune)
                        2) Bilateral hydrothorax
                        3) Prematurity – 35 weeks

D.O.B: March 18, 1994
Birth weight: 3320 grams   Length: 47.5 cm   HC: 34.5 cm
Gest. Age: 35.5 weeks AGA
DUBOWITZ: 35 weeks
APGARS: 2/3/5
Hospital of birth: MetroHealth Medical Center

Discharge Information:

Discharge Date: May 3, 1994
Discharge weight: 3270 grams   Length: 54 cm   HC: 34.5 cm
HCT: 28   *RETICS*: 1.6%
Age at time of discharge: 37 days old

Condition of patient at time of discharge: Good

Bethany's diagnoses and discharge information.

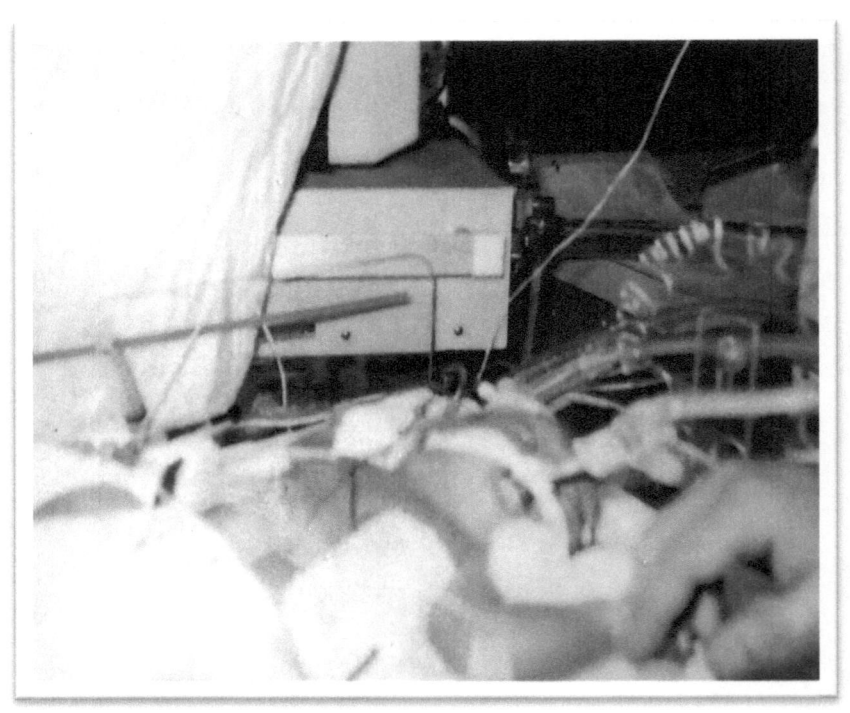

Day 2 of NICU.

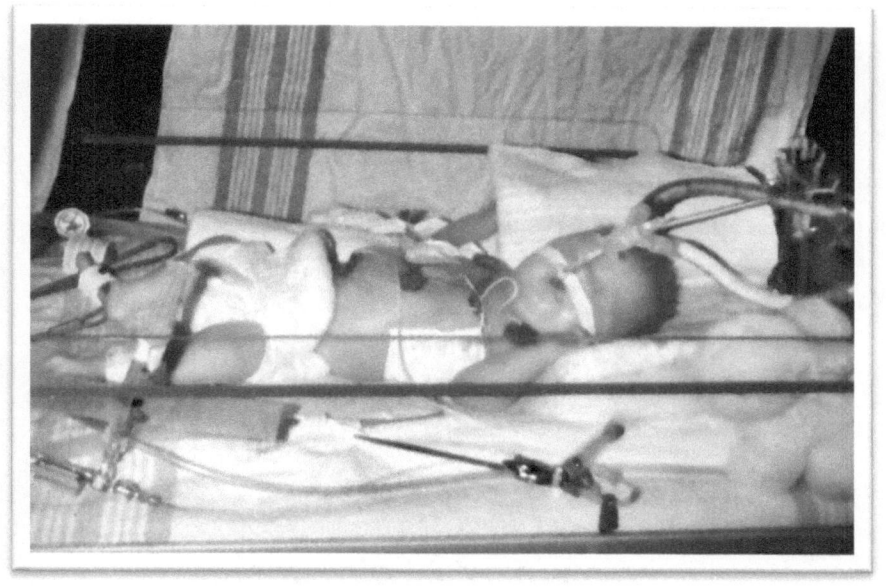

Day 5 of NICU. Some noticeable improvement.

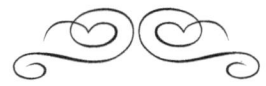

The Lord sustains them on
their sickbed
And restores them from
their bed of illness.

~ Psalms 41:3 N ~

Bethany's newborn portrait taken at 5 weeks old.

Healing through Faith

Lord, be merciful and gracious upon my
Child.

Please deliver my child from the clutches
Of sickness and death.

By Faith, I decree my child is made whole.

By Faith, I know my child will be healed
From her troubles.

Lord, by Faith, I command every spirit of
Sickness to be destroyed.

I pray for the Holy Spirit to take charge
Of the affairs of my child.

Because I know where your presence is,
Sickness cannot reside.

Thank you, Father, for healing my child.

Amen.

~ Faithful Christian ~

MORE TITLES FROM
DIRTY TRUTH PUBLISHING

*F.U.C.K. Your Insecurities!: The No-Bullshit Guide to
Stop Doubting Yourself, Be Who You Are, and
Do What You Want* (March 2021)

*Face It, You're Toxic!: How to Stop Negative Self Talk, Overcome
Insecurities and Feel Whole Again* (May 2021)

*Winning is For Losers!: How to Use Positive Thinking and the
Gift of Fear to Succeed in Life, Love and Business*
(September 2021)

*Stick with Your Own Kind!: How to Use Highly Effective People
to Achieve More and Live Better*
(December 2021)

*Speak Before You Think!: How to Talk to People, Listen with
Intention and Develop a Deep Connection*
(March 2022)

The Seeds of Greatness Are Within You: A Memoir
(November 2022)

*"Eye Can't" to I.C.O.N: A Journey of Transformation from
Visionless to Visionary* (November 2023)

*I'm Done Kissing Your Ass: True Stories and Life Lessons to
Ditch the Hero Worship and Discover Your Own Greatness.*
(April 2024)

All titles available for purchase at
www.dirtytruthpublishing.com